Rules and Recipes With a

Teacher's Book

by Carol Matchett
Pupil's Book by Stan Cullimore

Contents

Longman

Edinburgh Gate
Harlow, Essex

Rules for a Perfect Party and Recipe for a Perfect Summer Holiday

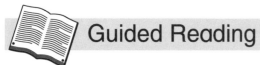 Guided Reading

Key Objectives

◆ Identify type of text, e.g. content, layout and purpose.

◆ Identify features of non-fiction texts, e.g. headings, lists, bullet points, captions.

Each child will need a set of labels cut out from Copymaster ❶.

Introduction

◆ Read the title of the book. *Is this book fiction or non-fiction? Ask the children to look through the book to confirm their predictions by referring to familiar non-fiction features.*

◆ Introduce the objectives for the session. Discuss the children's prior knowledge of rules and recipes. *What are rules? What rules are you familiar with? Why do we have them? What is a recipe? What does it tell you? When do you use one?* Establish that rules instruct you in what to do/how to behave, and that a recipe gives instructions for how to make something.

◆ Refer back to the title. *Why does the title say these are rules and recipes 'with a difference'?* Encourage the children to look through the headings and offer suggestions.

◆ Give each child a set of labels cut out from **Copymaster ❶**. Read through the labels with the children. Explain that non-fiction writers often use these features to help them set information out clearly. Discuss any terms that the children are unfamiliar with.

◆ Ask the children to find 'Rules for a Perfect Party'. *Read these rules. Think about what they tell you and how the information is set out. Use the arrow labels to point out the non-fiction features used by the author.*

Reading and Discussion

◆ Children read 'Rules for a Perfect Party' and label the text using the arrow cards.

◆ After reading, discuss the purpose and content of the rules. *What do these rules tell you? If you followed these rules would you have a perfect party? How are they different to the sort of rules you are familiar with?*

◆ Discuss which arrow labels the children have used [heading, list, numbered points, large print, bold print].

◆ Ask the children to repeat the procedure with 'Recipe for a Perfect Summer Holiday'.

◆ *What is the purpose of this recipe? Why is it different to a normal recipe? How is it similar to a normal recipe? If you followed this recipe would you have a perfect summer holiday?*

◆ Discuss the arrow labels the children have used [heading, sub-heading, list, bullet points, large print, bold print, etc.]

Returning to the Text for Evaluation and Analysis

◆ *How are these rules and recipes similar to other rules and recipes you have read?* [The purpose is the same; the layout features are familiar.] *How are they different?* [The content/subject is unusual.]

Reinforce the term instructions to describe this type of text.

◆ *What features of non-fiction texts did you find during reading?*

Rules for a Perfect Party and Recipe for a Perfect Summer Holiday

 Guided Writing

Key Objectives

◆ Write clear instructions using conventions learned from reading.

◆ Segment words into phonemes for spelling.

Task

Write a set of rules for a perfect summer holiday based on 'Rules for a Perfect Party'.

Each child will need Copymaster ❷ and a notebook or whiteboard and marker pen.

The teacher will need a whiteboard and marker pen.

Introduction

◆ Introduce the task and discuss the ideas included in 'Rules for a Perfect Party'. *What did you have to do to achieve a perfect party?*

◆ *What would make a perfect summer holiday?* Take suggestions from the children and scribe key words on the board, e.g. 'seaside', 'sunshine', 'swimming', 'beach', 'surfboard'. Involve the children in discussing spelling strategies while scribing, e.g.: *What letters make the 'ea'/'ur'/'oar' phoneme in this word?*

◆ Discuss how the 'Rules for a Perfect Party' were set out. *What features did the author use to make the rules easy to follow?* [Heading, list of numbered rules, use of bold print.]

◆ Give out **Copymaster ❷**. *This will help us to use the same features in our writing.*

◆ Read through the framework provided by the copymaster. Discuss ideas for some of the rules. *What should you remember to take with you?*

Children Writing Individually

◆ Ask the children to begin writing.

◆ Encourage the children to compose each rule orally before they write it down.

◆ Remind the children to use independent spelling strategies, e.g. segmenting words into phonemes, rather than copying words off the board. Invite the children to have a go at spelling words on their whiteboards or in their notebooks. *Check the spelling is correct before writing it on the copymaster.*

Evaluation

◆ Ask some of the children to read their work aloud. *Do these rules sound right? Would these rules help you to have a perfect summer holiday?* Identify any parts that don't sound right and discuss improvements.

◆ *What non-fiction text features have you used in your writing?*

◆ Ask the children to swap their work with a partner. *Can you see any words spelled incorrectly? Write the correct spelling on your whiteboard or in your notebook and show it to your partner.*

Suggested Independent Activities

◆ Collect examples of written rules to compare with those in the book.

◆ Read 'Rules about Picking Your Nose'.

◆ Write lists of 'Dos' and 'Don'ts'.

Features of Non-fiction Texts

Cut out these labels.

lists	captions
heading	sub-heading
numbered points	bullet points
text box	drawing
labelled diagram	large print
bold print	

Writing a Set of Rules

Write your own set of rules.

Rules for a Perfect Summer Holiday

Rule 1 Take _____

Rule 2 Don't forget _____

Rule 3 Have lots of _____

Rule 4 Play _____

Rule 5 Make sure _____

Rule 6 Don't _____

Rule 7 _____

Rule 8 _____

Rule 9 _____

Rule 10 _____

Recipe for a Water Fight and **Recipe for a Mud Pie**

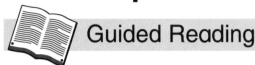 Guided Reading

Key Objective

◆ Identify features of instructional texts including: noting the intended outcome, listing materials or ingredients, clearly set out sequential stages, language of commands.

Each child will need Copymaster ❸.

Introduction

◆ Remind the children of the type of text found in this book. *Rules and recipes are types of instructions or instructional text. What is their purpose?* [To tell the reader how to do something.]

◆ Explain that the objective of the session is to identify the features of instructional texts. Give out **Copymaster ❸**. *This is the recipe we read in the last session.* Read through the recipe, identifying the features of instructional texts listed in the objective.

◆ Use questioning to establish how and why these features are used. *What is this recipe for? How do you know that?* [The heading establishes the intended outcome.] *Why are the ingredients listed at the start?* [So they can be collected together beforehand.] *Why is each step in the method separated out like this?* [To make it easier to follow.]

◆ Ask the children to read through the method on **Copymaster ❸** and circle each verb. *Remember verbs are the words that tell you what to do.* Check that the children are able to identify the verbs during this activity.

◆ When the activity is complete discuss the position of the verbs at the start of each step/bullet point. *This makes it sound like the writer is telling you directly what to do.*

◆ Tell the children that they are now going to read two other recipes in the book. *As you read them, see if these recipes have the same features.*

Reading and Discussion

◆ Children read 'Recipe for a Water Fight' and 'Recipe for a Mud Pie'.

◆ Support children where necessary, e.g. encouraging them to combine different cues when tackling unfamiliar words.

◆ Ask children to describe the familiar features of instructional texts. *Does this recipe have the same features as the other recipes you have read?*

◆ After reading, encourage children to respond to the content of the recipes. *What makes these recipes unusual? What is the intended outcome? Do you think we should take them seriously? What makes you say that?*

◆ Ask the children to identify the parts of the recipe they found particularly funny. Read those parts aloud.

Returning to the Text for Evaluation and Analysis

◆ *Did all of the recipes have the same text features?*

◆ *What did you notice about the verbs in the recipes? Were they always right at the start of each step?* [Sometimes they were preceded by a time connective, e.g. 'then', 'very soon'.]

◆ Review the main features of instructional texts identified during the session.

Recipe for a Water Fight and **Recipe for a Mud Pie**

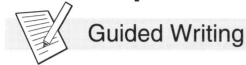 Guided Writing

Key Objective

◆ Write clear instructions using conventions learned from reading.

Task

Write a 'Recipe for a Snowball Fight' using 'Recipe from a Water Fight' as a model.

Each pair of children will need a set of pictures from Copymaster ❹ and *Rules and Recipes With a Difference*.
The teacher will need a whiteboard and marker pen.

Introduction

◆ Introduce the task and review the features of instructional texts/recipes as identified in the guided reading session.

◆ *How did 'Recipe for a Water Fight' start?* [With a heading that states the intended outcome.] *What came next?* [The sub-heading 'Ingredients' followed by a list of items.] Use the children's answers to form a framework on the board showing the heading ['Recipe for a Snowball Fight'], list of ingredients and method/series of steps.

◆ Discuss how a snowball fight might start. Give each pair of children a set of pictures from **Copymaster ❹**. *Put these pictures in order to show how the snowball fight developed.* Discuss the ordering of the pictures.

◆ Refer back to the framework on the board. *What ingredients might we list?* Look back at the list of ingredients in 'Recipe for a Water Fight'. Use this to suggest ideas, e.g. '1 cold snowy day'.

◆ Demonstrate how the steps in the original method can also be adapted and used in the new recipe, e.g. changing 'Wait for a hot sunny day' into 'Wait for a cold snowy day'.

Children Writing Individually

◆ Ask the children to begin writing by following the framework on the board. *How will you start? What should come next?*

◆ Use the pictures to identify the sequence of steps in the method.

◆ Remind the children to refer back to the original guided reading text to help write the method, e.g.: *What did the recipe say? What word/phrase did the writer start with? What parts can you use? What will you need to change?*

◆ Encourage the children to constantly reread their writing. *Does that sound right? Is it clear to the reader?*

Evaluation

◆ Read your recipe to your partner. *Has your partner followed the framework? Is each step in the method set out as a separate bullet point? Have they used verbs at the start of sentences to make it sound like instructions?*

◆ What have you learned about organising and writing instructions?

Suggested Independent Activities

◆ Collect examples of recipes to compare with those in the book. Are they all organised in the same way?

◆ Use a storyboard to show a sequence of steps in an activity, e.g. how to play a game, make something ...

◆ Represent the sequence of steps in one of the recipes on a flow chart.

Features of Instructions

Circle the verbs in the method.

Recipe for a perfect summer holiday

Ingredients:

1 family	a bag of buckets and spades
1 car	some money
1 holiday flat	lots of fresh air
1 seaside	lots of sunshine
50 litres of petrol	

Method:

▲ Get one family and one bag of buckets and spades.

▲ Put them in the car.

▲ Add 50 litres of petrol. (Put it in the petrol tank – NOT in the family.)

▲ Mix them well by driving for several hours.

▲ Take the family and bucket and spades out of the car.

▲ Place them in a holiday flat and let them cool down.

▲ Show them the seaside.

▲ Add the fresh air, sunshine and money.

▲ Now leave them alone for two weeks.

▲ At the end of this time they will have lots of good memories, suntans ... and a long drive back home!

Writing a Recipe for a Snowball Fight

Cut up these pictures and put them into the right order.

Rules to Keep Your Dog/Cat Happy and Rules to Keep on the Right/Wrong Side of Your Teacher

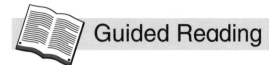 Guided Reading

Key Objectives

◆ Identify type of text, e.g. its content, layout and purpose.

◆ Examine headings that introduce content, capture interest.

Each pair of children will need a set of headings from Copymaster ❺.

Introduction

◆ Show the children the cover of the book and read the title. Don't let them open or look through the book at this point.

◆ Encourage predictions about the book's content based on the title. *What are rules and recipes? What is the purpose of them? Why do you think it says these are rules and recipes 'with a difference'?*

◆ Give out the headings from **Copymaster ❺**. Explain that these are taken from the book. *The heading can give us a good idea about the content of the text. What can you tell from these headings? Which do you most want to read?*

◆ Allow the children time to read and discuss the headings with their partner.

◆ Compare ideas. *Which of the headings captured your interest? Did any sound particularly useful? Did any just sound amusing?* Encourage children to explain their choices by making predictions about likely content.

◆ Ask for suggestions of how the rules and recipes might be set out based on prior knowledge of these forms. *Skim through the book to check your predictions.*

◆ Introduce the titles of the guided reading texts. Encourage the children to make predictions about the content, layout and purpose based on these titles.

◆ *Read 'Rules to Keep your Dog/Cat Happy'. See if your predictions are right.*

Reading and Discussion

◆ Draw the children's attention to the note written in brackets under the main headings.

◆ After reading, discuss similarities and differences. *What do you notice about these two sets of rules? What is the same?* [The organisation, layout, sentence structures …] *What has been changed?* [The purpose/stated aim.]

◆ *Do you think we are supposed to take these rules seriously? What makes you say that? Which parts do you find amusing?*

◆ If there is time, repeat the procedure with 'Rules to Keep on the Right/Wrong Side of Your Teacher'. Otherwise, ask the children to read these two texts independently prior to the guided writing session.

Returning to the Text for Evaluation and Analysis

◆ *What type of text have we been reading today?* [Establish that rules are an example of instructional texts.]

◆ *What was the purpose of these rules? Were the rules different to what you expected? Why?*

◆ *How can headings help the reader make predictions about the content, purpose and layout of a text?*

Rules to Keep Your Dog/Cat Happy and Rules to Keep on the Right/Wrong Side of Your Teacher

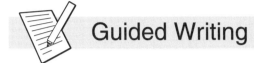 Guided Writing

Key Objective

◆ Write clear instructions using conventions learned from reading.

Task

Write two sets of rules called 'How to keep on the right/wrong side of your parent'.

Each child will need Copymaster ❻ and a notebook or whiteboard and marker pen.

Introduction

◆ Refer to the contrasting sets of rules in the guided reading text. Introduce the task. *What sort of things do you think we should include?* Discuss ideas for keeping on the right side of parents and for getting on their wrong side.

◆ *In 'Rules to Keep on the Right/Wrong Side of Your Teacher', what remained the same in both sets of rules and what was changed?* Clarify that the organisation, layout and language were the same, but the content changed to fit the right or wrong focus.

◆ Give out **Copymaster ❻**. Read the two rules provided. Remind the children that the 'wrong side of your parent' rules should be the opposite of these.

◆ Ask the children to try writing the opposite of rule number 1 on their whiteboards or in their notebooks. Prompt if necessary. *You could start: 'Don't bother to ...' or 'Never ...'*

◆ Encourage the children to add a further comment to their new rule, e.g. suggesting what the reader could do instead. *Start a new sentence with the words 'Instead, spend the time ...'*

◆ When the children are happy with their version of rule 1 this can be written on the copymaster.

Children Writing Individually

◆ Ask the children to repeat the process with rule 2.

◆ Remind the children to use a comma between the two parts of the sentence in rule 2.

◆ Encourage children to read each rule aloud to a partner in the group. *Does it sound right? Can it be improved? Can the idea be developed more?* Transfer the completed rules to the copymaster.

◆ Help the children to form their own ideas for rules 3 and 4. *How might you start?* Suggest possibilities e.g. 'Never ...', 'Always ...', 'Do ...', 'Don't ...', 'When you come home ...' 'In the evening ...'.

Evaluation

◆ Ask some of the children to read their work aloud. *Do these rules sound right? Are they amusing? Could any of the rules be developed further?*

◆ What words make them sound like rules? ['Always', 'never', 'do', 'don't'.]

Suggested Independent Activities

◆ Read 'Rules about Burping in Public'.

◆ Write your own list of 'Dos' and 'Don'ts' relating to behaviour in assembly, when watching television, on a bus, in a cinema ...

What Does the Heading Tell Us?

What do these headings tell you about the text that follows?

Rules for a Perfect Party

Recipe for a Perfect Summer Holiday

Rules about Picking Your Nose

Recipe for a Water Fight

Recipe for a Mud Pie

Rules to Keep Your Dog Happy

Rules to Keep Your Cat Happy

Recipe for a Pocket Money Rise

Rules to Keep on the *Right* Side of Your Teacher

Rules to Keep on the *Wrong* Side of Your Teacher

Rules About Burping in Public

Recipe for a Perfect School Day

Rules to Keep Your Bedroom Looking Tidy

Rules to Make You Rich

Writing Contrasting Sets of Rules

Write your own set of rules.

Rules to Keep on the *Right* Side of Your Parent

Rule 1   Wash up all of the breakfast things every morning.

Rule 2   When you leave the house in the morning, always thank your parent for the packed lunch/clean PE kit/ lovely breakfast.

Rule 3 _____

_____

Rule 4 _____

_____

Rules to Keep on the *Wrong* Side of Your Parent

Rule 1 _____

_____

Rule 2 _____

_____

Rule 3 _____

_____

Rule 4 _____

_____

Recipe for a Pocket Money Rise and Recipe for a Perfect School Day

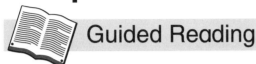 Guided Reading

Key Objective

◆ Identify features of instructional texts including: noting the intended outcome at the beginning, listing ingredients, clearly set out sequential stages, language of commands.

Each child will need a copy of Copymaster ❼.

The teacher will need a flipchart or whiteboard and marker pen.

Introduction

◆ Introduce the purpose of the session: to identify features of instructional texts and decide why they are written in this way.

◆ Introduce the titles of the two recipes. *What makes these recipes different to other recipes you have read?*

◆ Explain that although they are unusual subjects for a recipe, they still use the same features as other instructional texts.

◆ *Look at how these recipes are organised. What features make them look like a recipe?* [The heading stating what is being made or achieved; the layout, e.g. the list of ingredients, the sequence of stages or steps in the method; the use of illustrations to support.] List these points on the board.

◆ Discuss why each of these features is needed, for example: *Why is it important to list the ingredients at the start of the recipe? Why are the stages in the method separated out?*

◆ Ask the children to read 'Recipe for a Pocket Money Rise'. *As you read, think about how the language used makes this sound like a set of instructions from a real recipe.*

Reading and Discussion

◆ Children read pages 14 and 15.

◆ Explain the use of 'NB' when adding an important note for the reader.

◆ After reading, discuss the content of the recipe. *Do you think this recipe would work in your house? Are we meant to take the recipe seriously? Which parts did you find amusing?*

◆ Discuss the instructional-style language used in the recipe, e.g. the use of imperative verbs ('rush', 'place', 'wait') and time related phrases ('after a few minutes', 'now'). Locate examples, and list them on the board.

◆ Discuss how the basic instructions are elaborated for the reader. *Why has the author added the safety warning? What does the extra information in brackets tell the reader? Why does the writer give an example of a good reason?*

◆ If there is time, give out **Copymaster ❼**, which features 'Recipe for a Perfect School Day'. Ask the children to complete the labels and highlight the imperative verbs and time connectives. Otherwise this can be completed as an independent activity.

Returning to the Text for Evaluation and Analysis

◆ *What have you learned about the features of instructional texts? How are they organised? What sort of language is used?*

◆ Make sure the main features are listed on the board.

Recipe for a Pocket Money Rise and Recipe for a Perfect School Day

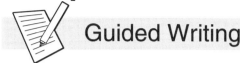 Guided Writing

Key Objectives

◆ Write clear instructions using conventions learned from reading, including link phrases, organisational devices.

◆ Use verb tense appropriate to type of text.

Task

Write a 'Recipe for My Perfect Saturday' based on the diary notes on **Copymaster ❽**.

Each child will need Copymaster ❽.

The teacher will need a whiteboard and marker pen, and the list of features made during the guided reading session.

Introduction

◆ Introduce the task. Discuss ideas for what makes a perfect Saturday. *What ingredients would you have in your perfect Saturday?*

◆ Remind the group of the instructional text features identified during the guided reading session. Refer to the list on the board. *This will remind us how to organise the recipe and the sort of language to use.*

◆ Give out **Copymaster ❽**. Explain that these are notes from a diary. Read the notes. *Do they sound like instructions? Why not?* Establish that a diary says what happened, rather than instructing what to do.

◆ *How can I change 'Woke up really late' into an instruction?* Establish that the verb needs to be changed. Write 'Wake up really late' on the board. *This is now an instruction.*

Children Writing Individually

◆ Tell the children to begin by writing a heading and list of ingredients for the recipe.

◆ When the children are writing the method, check they change the verbs into the imperative form.

◆ Remind them to use time connectives to provide links between the various steps.

Refer to examples on the copymaster, e.g. 'now', 'eventually', 'when'.

◆ At a suitable point, stop the group to discuss how adding further comments will help develop the basic instructions. Remind the children how this was achieved in the guided reading text, e.g. by using brackets, examples, NB.

◆ *What could we add to 'Wake up really late?'* Discuss possibilities, for example: 'NB Not too late or you will miss most of the day'.

◆ Ask the children to extend at least one of their instructions in this way.

Evaluation

◆ Is your writing organised like a recipe?

◆ Does it sound like a recipe? Try reading it aloud. Are there any parts you can improve or add to?

◆ What have you learned about the language used in instructional texts? What sorts of verbs are used?

Suggested Independent Activities

◆ Make a collection of recipes from magazines. Label them to show the organisation and language features.

◆ Write your own perfect day recipe.

Features of Instructional Texts

1 Complete the labels.

2 Highlight all of the **verbs** in one colour.

3 Highlight **time connectives** in a different colour.

Recipe for a Perfect School Day

Ingredients:

1 school day

a small pinch

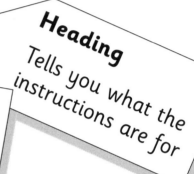

Heading
Tells you what the instructions are for

Method:

1 Wake up – late.

Allow your parents to bring you breakfast in bed.

Lie in bed and watch television for a few hours.

Get up eventually and dress.

Get a taxi to the park to hang out with your friends.

Buy several ice creams and eat them.

Return home to play a few computer games.

Order a takeaway pizza for tea.

Spend the evening watching videos and texting your friends.

Finally, go to bed.

2 Now, pinch yourself and wake up! Remember – you are a child, you HAVE to go to school!

Writing Instructions

Write a 'Recipe for a Perfect Saturday' based on these notes from a diary.

Saturday

Had a really great day...

Woke up really late

Watched television in bed

Got up late and had breakfast

Played computer games

Called for my friends

Cycled to the park

Had fun

Bought ice creams and drinks

Cycled home

Ordered takeaway pizza for tea

Went to cinema

Watched television

Went to bed

When you write your recipe try to include some time connectives to link the instructions together.

First	**Eventually**	**After a while**
Now	**When**	**Finally**

Rules to Keep Your Bedroom Looking Tidy, Rules to Make You Rich/Poor and Recipe for World Peace

 Guided Reading

Key Objective

◆ Identify type of text, e.g. content, structure, vocabulary, style, layout and purpose.

Each pair of children will need a set of statements and style words from Copymaster ❾.

Introduction

◆ Read the title of the book. *What do you know about rules and recipes? What sort of text are they? What is their purpose?* Establish that rules and recipes are examples of instructional texts that seek to help the reader achieve a stated outcome.

◆ Ask the children to explain how they would expect to find a recipe or a set of rules organised/set out. *Have a look through the book. Are these set out in that way?* Encourage the children to identify familiar features, e.g. lists of ingredients, use of bullet points or numbered lists.

◆ *The title says 'Rules and Recipes with a Difference'. Have you noticed anything unusual about these rules and recipes?* Ask the children to read the list of headings on the contents page. Invite comments from the children about the unusual content.

◆ Put the children into pairs and give each pair a set of statement cards from **Copymaster ❾**. *These statements describe reasons why an author might write a set of instructions. You are going to read four sets of instructions and decide on the author's purpose for writing them.*

◆ Direct the children to find pages 24–27.

Reading and Discussion

◆ The children read each set of instructions and discuss with their partner the most likely purpose.

◆ When the reading is complete compare ideas. *What was the author's main purpose when writing 'Rules to Keep Your Bedroom Looking Tidy'?* [To make you smile.] *How can you tell? Are these instructions really useful for keeping your bedroom tidy?*

◆ *Why do you think the author wrote 'Recipe for World Peace'?* [To make the reader think.] *What makes you say that? Find the parts that make you think? What does it make you think about?*

◆ Give out the sets of style words from the copymaster. Which of these words would you use to describe each set of instructions you have read? Allow the children time to discuss this with their partner before reporting back.

◆ Ask the children to justify their choice of style words by referring to examples of words or phrases from the text.

Returning to the Text for Evaluation and Analysis

◆ *What was unusual about these rules and recipes? What was familiar?* [The structure, layout and language.] *What was different?* [Content, style and purpose.]

◆ *How has the author used the instructional form to make you smile or to make you think?*

Rules to Keep Your Bedroom Looking Tidy

 Guided Writing

Key Objectives

◆ Write clear instructions using conventions learned from reading.

◆ Use commas to mark grammatical boundaries in sentences.

Task

Write 'Rules to keep the classroom looking tidy' using the guided reading text as a model.

Each child will need a notebook or whiteboard and marker pen, and *Rules and Recipes With a Difference*.
The teacher will need a whiteboard and marker pen.

Introduction

◆ Introduce the task and discuss the author's purpose when writing the guided reading text, i.e. to amuse the reader. *We are going to make our rules amusing, rather than serious.*

◆ Discuss ideas for the classroom rules. *What sort of mess do we have in the classroom?* [Half-eaten packets of crisps, pencil sharpenings, PE kits.] *Where does this tend to get hidden?* [In trays, desks, the art cupboard.]

◆ Ask the children to find the guided reading text. *Look at how each of the first four rules starts with the phrase, 'If you have any …'*

◆ Demonstrate how to use this sentence structure to form a rule for the classroom. Write on the board 'If you have any dirty, smelly PE kit that needs washing …' Ask the children to complete this sentence on their whiteboards or in their notebooks. Compare ideas.

◆ Point out the position of the two commas: one between the two adjectives, and one between the two parts of the sentence.

◆ Ask the children to begin writing their own list of rules. *Number your rules as Rule 1, Rule 2, etc. You can start each rule with the phrase, 'If you have any …'*

Children Writing Individually

◆ The children can try out their sentences on the whiteboard or in their notebook before writing them on paper.

◆ Encourage the children to develop ideas using sentence constructions suggested by the guided reading text, e.g. 'don't throw it in the bin because …', 'instead …', 'otherwise …'

◆ Check that the children use commas appropriately in their sentences.

◆ Encourage children to develop ideas for the last rule. *What suggestions might you offer for when the classroom is really untidy?*

Evaluation

◆ Ask some of the children to read their rules aloud. *Does this work? Is it amusing? Does it sound and look like a real set of rules? Why?*

◆ *Where have you used commas in your sentences? Why were they needed?*

Suggested Independent Activities

◆ Use **Copymaster ❿** and the cards from **Copymaster ❾** to assess the purpose and style of other instructional texts.

◆ Write rules that might *really* help to keep your bedroom tidy.

Author's Purpose and Style

Cut out these statements and words.

Statements to describe an author's purpose:

> **to make you smile**

> **to make you think**

> **to help you make something**

> **to help you complete a task successfully**

> **to help you find your way**

> **to tell you what to do**

Words to describe an author's style:

> **jokey**   **serious**   **thoughtful**

> **humorous**   **formal**   **friendly**

> **technical**

Author's Purpose and Style

Complete this table to compare the purpose and style of instructional texts.

Title of text	Purpose	Style

Recipe for a Long and Happy Life/Keeping Your Friends and Rules for Dealing With Aliens

 Guided Reading

Key Objective

◆ Identify features of instructional texts including: noting the intended outcome, listing materials or ingredients, clearly set out sequential stages, language of commands.

Each child will need a notebook or whiteboard and marker pen and Copymaster ⓫.

Introduction

◆ Introduce the purpose of the session. *These aren't real instructions, but they do look and sound like instructions.*

◆ *What features of instructional texts does this book use?* Invite the children to look through the book and identify familiar organisational features, e.g. a heading that states what the instructions are for, lists of ingredients, a clear sequence of stages. Identify how these stages are made clear, e.g. lists, numbering, bullet points.

◆ Discuss how rules are organised differently to recipes. *Why is there no list of ingredients with the rules? Do rules always have to be followed in order?*

◆ Focus on the language features of instructional texts. Refer back to 'Recipe for World Peace' to help illustrate. Point out the use of imperative verbs, e.g. 'take', 'place', 'allow', and time connectives, e.g. 'now', 'then'.

◆ Ask the children to read the three guided reading texts and to record on their whiteboards, or in their notebooks, examples of typical instructional language.

Reading and Discussion

◆ Encourage the children to respond to the subject matter of each text e.g.: *How does 'Recipe for a Long and Happy Life' make you feel? Why?*

◆ As the children proceed with their reading, discuss the imperative verbs and time connectives noted.

◆ Discuss whether 'Rules for Dealing with Aliens' uses time connectives/imperative verbs in the same way as the other texts. *Why is this different?*

◆ After the children have read all three texts, encourage comparisons in terms of purpose. *Which were written to make you think? Which are meant to be amusing?*

◆ Identify examples of cookery-style language used in 'Recipe for Keeping your friends', e.g. the choice of verbs ('mix', 'serve') and measurements ('a pinch', 'a teaspoon'). *Why does the author use this style of language?*

◆ If time, the children should complete **Copymaster ⓫** to reinforce the language features of instructional texts. Otherwise this can be set as an independent activity.

Returning to the Text for Evaluation and Analysis

◆ Revise the main features identified during the session. *How were the instructions organised? What language features made them sound like real instructions?*

◆ Ask the children to work with a partner. *Write a checklist of things to remember when writing instructions.* Make one list of points under the heading 'Organisation', and one list of points under the heading 'Language'.

◆ Compare checklists. Compose a complete group version that can be used during the guided writing session.

Recipe for a Long and Happy Life and Recipe for Keeping Your Friends

 Guided Writing

Key Objectives

◆ Write clear instructions using conventions from reading.

◆ Improve the cohesion of written instructions through the use of link phrases and organisational devices.

Task

Write a recipe for a happy school.

Each child will need Copymaster ⑫, *Rules and Recipes With a Difference* and paper for writing and for presentation.

Introduction

◆ Review the purpose of the two recipes read in the guided reading session. *What was the message of each recipe?*

◆ Introduce the task. *We are going to write our own recipe with a message. It will be organised and set out just like any other recipe – but it will make everyone in the school think about how they can help achieve a happy school.*

◆ Discuss possible 'ingredients' for a happy school.

◆ Give out copies of **Copymaster ⑫** (or you can use the school's own rules if you prefer). Read and discuss the statements. *Do you agree with them? Are there any others you wish to add?*

◆ Explain that these statements tell people how to behave, but they are not written as a recipe. *How could we make these look more like a recipe? How does a recipe start? How is it organised?* [A heading stating the intended outcome, 'Ingredients', 'Method'.]

◆ *What sort of language should we use?* Remind the children to use measurements, imperative verbs and time connectives.

Children Writing Individually

◆ The children begin by composing their heading and list of ingredients.

◆ Encourage the use of time connectives to join the steps together in the method, e.g. 'First …', 'Now …'

◆ Remind the children to use cookery terms, particularly verbs, e.g. 'Add', 'Stir', and measurements such as 'a pinch of …'

◆ Refer the children back to sentence constructions used in 'Recipe for Keeping Your Friends', e.g.: *Could you continue that sentence by using a dash?* Or try using the phrase 'remembering to …'

Evaluation

◆ Ask the children to use the checklist formed in the guided reading session to evaluate their own writing. *Have you organised your writing properly? Have you used language features effectively?*

◆ Select some examples to read aloud. *Does this sound like a recipe? What works well? What could be improved? Is the message clear?*

◆ How shall we present our recipes to the rest of the school?

Suggested Independent Activities

◆ Use ICT to help present the recipe for use in the school.

◆ Collect examples of other instructional texts and analyse the features used.

Features of Instructional Texts

Highlight the verbs in this recipe.
Circle the time connectives.

Recipe for World Peace

Method:

Take the human race and remove all greed. Now remove all racism, sexism and intolerance.

Place the human race on the face of the Earth.
Allow them to live and love, wherever and whoever they wish.
Allow them to worship the god of their choice.

Now take one pinch of hope and leave the mix to settle.

Then serve.

Highlight all the words and phrases that make this sound like a cookery recipe.

Recipe for Keeping Your Friends

Method:

☺ Take one measure of kindness, remembering to use the same amount as you would like to have used on you.

☺ Add a pinch of patience – especially when your friends are going on about something that you find boring.

☺ Stir in a touch of tolerance – everyone has the right to their own opinions.

☺ Add a teaspoon of truth, bearing in mind that too much can be harmful!

☺ Mix well and leave to stand.

☺ Serve with a sprinkle of apologies whenever they are needed.